(he)art.

zane frederick

(he)art.

Printed in the United States of America.

ISBN-13: 978-1975853136

ISBN-10: 197585313X

Edited by Kama O'Connor
Cover art by Michele Spurza

zane frederick

acknowledgements

to my parents, who taught me everything i know. thank you for loving me in every way there is to love. you showed me how to live and enjoy life, despite her ugly moments. thank you both for making me from scratch, without your magic, this book would not be here.

to my sister, you taught me how to be the best version of myself possible. you showed me that love is never going to be perfect and pretty, it is going to be ugly and painful and unforgettable. most importantly, you made me brave, and i can't thank you enough for that.

to my friends, you all have shown me what it is to be loved, supported, and appreciated, without judgment, without hesitation, without doubt. thank you for making me laugh until my lungs went numb and my jaw sore. you have been there since the beginning, and i thank you a thousand times.

to my readers, i want this book to be your therapist, your best friend, your sense of validation for the chaos inside of your mind. i hope you find comfort in these words the same way that i have. i hope you find some peace in here. keep reading. keep loving.

(he)art.

to the one who inspired most of these confessions,

thank you.

these are the words i never truly said to you. hidden in fear of
your reaction, or that you would make me transparent enough
to see what i was thinking of. granted, these words have aged
since the time they were written on napkins or in iphone notes
and so has the meaning. these words are no longer attached to
you, however, they remain the answers to questions i asked
myself, and perhaps the answers you never had questions for.

you came at the right time in my life and made everything
better, even when you managed to simultaneously make
everything worse. thanks for being a firework.

i hope you're well.

with love,

me

zane frederick

contents

(he)art.

zane frederick

BLEEDING

(he)art.

the truth

my writings

hold the truth

all the words

i was too afraid

to say to you

normal

as a young boy
i never thought of myself
as normal
or human
someone who would grow
to hate seafood
and camping
someone who would
eventually fall into the category
of the hopeless romantics
or who would find love
in someone of similar skin
and composition
but eventually learn to look
in the mirror
smile at the quirks
and be human enough
to say
i am normal
that i am
my own version of love

(he)art.

crimson

a heart so pure

untouched by fire

but i have found matches

to do enough damage

eighteen months later

before it gets good

i am an unreliable lover

known as the flight risk

the one who runs away

at any sign of interest

or finds the flaw in any love

as a means of escape

too afraid for

any possibilities to show

too afraid for

any flowers to grow

(he)art.

battles with the body
finding love for
not only a boy
but for me
was my body's own
civil war
a battlefield of
scratches and scars
until my heart
gave up the fight
laid his armor down
to allow a love between
myself
and someone else
come together
in something tender
and fragile
with the potential to be
something big
and beautiful

my blue

i love the color blue

and all shades of it

from clear skies

to orchids

though his blue

is my favorite

(he)art.

yellow lights

you came out of nowhere

though i should not

be surprised

i switch lanes

without blinkers

speed up

at yellow lights

you were a deer

in the road

and i never

saw you coming

welcome home pt. i

something was different that day

the air felt clearer

reeked of innocence

his arms welcomed me home

and my bags were packed

i moved into his mind

i used to visit it

but now

i live in it

(he)art.

predictable

he was curious

and kind

and mysterious

the way he held

that smug look on his face

like he knew everything

about me

like he somehow knew

he was capable

of destroying me

keep glowing

you shined that
flashlight smile at me
the kind that lingered on
when you close your eyes
like the feeling of staring
at the sun too long

(he)art.

the little things
you learn to fall for
the minor details
the little things
like the way he laughs
and the way he breathes
and the way he looks
when he falls asleep

left handed

you moved your hands on me

like cursive

and i just have

bad handwriting

(he)art.

the touch

i felt your breath on me

that sunday evening

a breath that held

the scent of lust

like you wanted me

to kiss you

the type of breath

you feel

right before

the touch

welcome home pt. ii

i spread my ribs

cracking every bone

trying to make more space for you

to build you a home

because you're a warm fireplace

lighting up the room

and i realized home sure felt

a hell of a lot like you

(he)art.

(he)art.

you are the first thing

that has made the word

"love"

feel exactly

what it sounds like

#@%&

your name

is the kind of

heart stopping

stomach dropping

curse word

my favorite noun

and the sweetest sound

(he)art.

coincidence

i call you love

like it is your first name

but love is a four letter word

and so is yours

i think there's

a coincidence here

all over

love came to me

like wind

a rush of something

oddly familiar

felt good against my skin

and through the twists in my hair

i felt this love

all the time

i felt this love

everywhere

(he)art.

prisoner

your name escapes

from my teeth

like a jail cell

your mouth

is like family

and your lips

are always welcome

to visit

love me all the time

at night is when you

decide to love me

you come out of your skin

and settle in me like

i was the one thing

that kept you warm in this life

so love me tonight

and make this promise for me

that you will still love me

in the dark

and in the morning

(he)art.

red

we smoked a little too much that evening

the moon laughed at our madness

your eyes were so red that night

as i started to fall again

in a whole new color

a brand new light

fade into you

you hug

like a black hole

you pull me in

you swallow

(he)art.

angles

i stared at you

all night

you looked beautiful

at every angle

come home

when you said "come home"

did you mean to phoenix

on fourteenth avenue?

or did you mean somewhere else

somewhere next to you?

(he)art.

the word

i want to scream it

from roof tops

and parking lots

to bedroom floors

and grocery stores

i want to say it out loud

but my mouth was raised

to be still in these moments

i know you can't read my mind

but i'm hoping you can read my eyes

play me a song

it wasn't your laugh

it was *the way* you laughed

how you made music

with your xylophone ribs

and formed crinkles in your cheeks

just like a little kid

(he)art.

the crinkles were loud
we loved in a car where
the silences were comfortable
with words that never
had to be spoke
we loved in a car where
i heard your smile
after each punchline
like i could feel your love
on every drive home

confused fingers

i wonder if you felt something

when we brushed our hands

i wonder if you are just

as confused

as i am

(he)art.

save me

i'm not sure if i'll be fine

or if i'll make it out alive

because i believe

you're a deadly disease

and the antidote

all at the same time

the view

he said the hike was worth it

and i never put so much trust

in a boy and my lungs until

we made it to the top

and i stopped to look at the view

it was absolutely breathtaking

all of the lights

and you

(he)art.

practice

i was never one to

confess my feelings

or admit them out loud

told my friends

i had a little crush

but they knew before i did

the love spilled

from my eyes

as i looked at yours

screamed from my mouth

when i said hello

held on to your skin

after letting go

the risks are worth it

go ahead and break me

i won't mind

(he)art.

collision

i picture us

crashing into each other

like a tidal wave

or a car accident

and i would risk

not wearing a life vest

or a seatbelt

if it meant i got to come into

any type of contact

with you

us

all my stories

start

and

end

with

you

(he)art.

zane frederick

BRUISING

(he)art.

city of love

there's a city called love

i like to drive in at night

but i keep running into potholes

and hitting all the red lights

gay pt. i

the word

was thrown at me

like stones

the label

had been shoved

down my throat

before i was even

given the chance

to become it

(he)art.

determination

loving you was
learning to ride a bike
always falling off
always getting back on

closed

he was a door that said pull

but i kept pushing him

and no matter how hard i tried

he never let me in

(he)art.

show me the stars
your freckles
were constellations
of stars
i could not reach
i tried building a ladder
that was high enough
to get a closer look
but you ended up being taller
than all the monsters i
became friends with
and every night
we would celebrate
have a big slumber party
under my bed
sharing nightmares
and our biggest fears
even they
are afraid of you

2 a.m. thoughts

i believed the thoughts between us

were something for sure

but while i was thinking of you

you were thinking of her

(he)art.

jenga

you pulled pieces out of me
as if i would not be weakened
attempted to see
how much you could remove
before i became fragile enough
to come crashing down

reserved

if my tiny hips
are too small to fit
into the parking lot
of your pelvis
why would i be a love
you want to be with

(he)art.

nighttime

i can feel the sadness
i'm starting to choke
up the broken pieces
that are in my throat
i better close my eyes
before the tears start
i better fall asleep
before i fall apart

you never really liked art museums

to other men

i was art

they could look

but they could not touch

and as soon as you laid

your eyes on me

i could tell you loved

breaking the rules

so with your match like fingers

you managed to burn out

every masterpiece you touched

and when you got to me

you caressed every inch

of my canvas body

until i was scarred

in your unrequited love

but i do not regret you

breaking the rules

and even though

i'm a little charred

you are still my favorite

piece in the room

(he)art.

masterpiece

your hands looked crafted

carved like a marble sculpture

but you destroyed a masterpiece

when i watched you hold hers

no i don't (yes i do)

i lied to you

the first time you asked

if i loved anyone

and i never wanted to lie

but i guess we both broke promises

(he)art.

stop, drop, and roll

you setup a campsite

inside of my head

but forgot to put out the fire

when you packed up and left

you caused a forest fire in my mind

and i'm not sure how to put it out

every now and then

my love for you

comes in waves

like a summer breeze

or a stomach ache

(he)art.

tylenol before bed
remembering him
came back in pieces
like a sunday hangover
recalling memories
of last night's mistakes
to remind you how it felt
to get drunk off
his artificial love
then throwing it all up
the next morning

i am not her

he told me he had never

seen someone

quite like her

someone with those eyes

those set of hands

someone he prefers

(he)art.

home in heartbreak

i found a love who

put a broken home

in a crooked smile

i felt secure with him

even in the hurt

i felt safe

in a dangerous place

sweet sting

like a bee

your name

still stings

still buzzes

around me

but just like

honey

it is still

so sweet

(he)art.

prom

i still recall the night

of you wearing your suit

those eyes and black bow tie

and too much perfume

when i thought that you loved me

i should have never assumed

please tell me why are

you leaving so soon?

close your eyes
you don't mind
loving me
in disguise
when it goes dark
after hours
just as long
as the world
is sound asleep
just as long
as no one sees

(he)art.

the possibility of us
you did not stay because
i think you were afraid
of falling for me
terrified of
the possibility of us
so you did
what you always do best
packed all your things
took a piece of me
and left

may

i saved the nights for you

the moon was your favorite

the stars cheered us on

but just like you

the moon left too

so now my nights feel empty

down our favorite avenue

(he)art.

queen sized sadness

i never noticed how big

my bed used to be

until i saw your absence

sleeping

on the other side of me

elevator music

maybe we're supposed
to end up together
as cliché as it sounds
but i don't know how
i could live my life
without you
in the background

(he)art.

space
if you want space
i would fly to the moon and back
sacrificing light years without you
because you wanted space
if you want space
i would smash the keyboard
until my fingers form calluses
because you wanted space
if you want space
then i'll leave you alone
hoping
waiting
for you to return
because you wanted space

a handful of me

i gave you everything
handed you pieces of me
you did not ask for
and when your pockets got full
you let my petals drop
decomposing in the soil
of an unwatered love

(he)art.

the absence of happiness

i am not cold

just an absence

of heat

i am not sad

just an absence

of you

be back by morning

i watched a love walk away

like a sunset

so light for so long

darkness is on the horizon

and i can't see a thing

a love who hid

behind the earth

in search for something

less draining than me

a love that no longer

is rich and sweet

so while i wait

for the moon to leave

and the darkness to end

i pray that by tomorrow

he comes around again

(he)art.

all gone

i forget how empty i am

a sink with broken pipes

i have drained myself

of all the love i tried

to fill in someone

who did not have

the desire

to thirst on

boom

sometimes i think

i'm a bomb

ready to explode

at any second

and maybe that's why

i push people away

i don't want them to be

anywhere near me

because when i go off

i don't want them

to have to pick up the pieces

of a mess i made

even if they want to help

i don't want to hurt them

along the way

(he)art.

thump thump

is that the sound

of my heart

beating

or breaking?

friday nights

i drank to forget about you

tried to drown out the memory

of you leaving me

thinking it wouldn't hurt

but the pain felt the same

and by the end of the night

even the vodka

left me too

(he)art.

her ignorance

the night you told me
you kissed her
felt like every building
in my stomach
collapsing at the same time
being paralyzed in a smile
pretending to be happy
while being mad at her
for she does not know
how your lips velcro together
like light up shoes
a bright smile
without showing teeth
a sweetness in every smirk
how she does not know
the freckle that lives
on your bottom lip
and how mine would love
to meet him one day

prized possessions

to him she was gold

with sun blonde hair

and eyes like a riptide

she pulled him back

to him i was silver

with platinum blonde hair

and eyes like a fool

he did not want

someone like me

lesser quality

though for him

i tried to be

everything

(he)art.

coming out

there is no need to rush
when loving yourself
inside you will figure out
everything you need to know
step out when you're ready
bring a sword in both hands
make pride in vulnerability

under construction

i was doing fine

before you came along

bulldozed into my life

as if i needed to change

a renovation of my heart

though this skyscraper body

is not done yet

you and i

are unfinished business

(he)art.

breaking and entering

your love

comes and goes

like a robbery

taking the things

you want

and leaving

all the broken pieces

with me

the hurt

all those times

i was to you

someone to use

or lie to

it all hurt

but i wanted you

that was the issue

i confused the hurt

as a false sense

of desire

mistook your

sharp hands

as soft skin

bled love

every time

you touched me

but never wanted

those wounds to heal

in hindsight

i kind of liked the burn

(he)art.

are you there?

i miss you

the kind of *i miss you*

when you are next to me

yet feel so far away

the kind of *i miss you*

when i hear your name

and search for you

the kind of *i miss you*

when i want to say

i love you

but all that spills is

goodbye

the kind of *i miss you*

when i want to call home

but know you will no longer

answer the phone

checking up

how do i not

check up on you?

how do i not

make sure

that you still

don't love me?

(he)art.

waiting

they say

the pain

will be worth it

in the end

but when is

the end?

when did it

begin?

retreat

i close into myself

a rose

too afraid

to come undone

(he)art.

closed doors

i think i'm afraid

to let people in

because i would be

giving them the opportunity

to walk out

pieces

i have become accustomed

to sharing parts of myself

to temporary lovers

thinking i would

get something

in return

but end up giving

the right pieces

to the wrong person

(he)art.

vacancy

i'm afraid

i will not be good at it

loving someone

who loves me

i am scared to find

a new version of home

because when a love

becomes vacant

i worry as if i won't

be enough

to occupy it

transparent

this body

is an abandoned warehouse

with open doors

and broken windows

you could see

everything inside

and after attempting

to board up wounds

left from those

who ran with scissors

i realized that

these fractured bones

can't heal on their own

and i worry

that i can't fix this body

that i am an old skyscraper

ready to collapse

that would take years

of construction

before i ever came back

i worry

that this body

is not enough

for any body

(he)art.

do not grow small for someone

i'm not sure if

i still love you

because i'm afraid to let go

or if i really do feel

that fiery burn

and i fear that it's

an awful mixture of both

because even

in a crowded room

i could still find you

yet feel so small

so minuscule

like a waste of your space

had me wrapped

around your finger

in the palm of your hand

molded me down

small enough to walk past

without turning around

but look at me

i am screaming at you

someone help me

get big again

leave a message

i'm starting to forget

what your voice sounds like

the warm tone

that kept me

from the cold

and left goosebumps

with every whisper

i miss you

but i am too afraid

to call you

and listen to the way

you say my name

and lose all the progress

that i have made

(he)art.

abandoned

do not start something

if you are not going to finish

but how can i complain

if you were never mine

to begin with

finished

our love was rare
at least i like to think so
when we reached for the stars
without even jumping
when we danced in a language
only we spoke
touched each other
like colliding flames
and fought
in the same exact way
you made
a forest fire out of me
and there was always
that spark in your eyes
i saw it no doubt
we seemed like
the perfect match
right before we burned out

(he)art.

leave my mind
i'm sorry that you are still the subject
of most of my rhymes
but i can only seem to write about
your lips against mine
and i have been trying to write
about something new
but there are still things i never
got to say to you
like how i love
the way your hair
falls over your face
and how i want to know
how you laugh and think
and how your lips taste

bookmarked

i read poetry books

hoping to find answers in the words

answers to your sweet disposition

and the times i felt unsure

maybe that's why

all the pages are cornered

why i leave my books unfinished

because i believe

we're a never ending story

with just a bookmark in it

(he)art.

9 months later

you birth smiles out of me
like they have been growing
in my mouth for months
and that is terrifying
knowing you can pull
happiness out of me
when i didn't even know
it was there

blue and you

i need to meet

a new love with

green eyes

brown eyes

grey eyes

any color

besides

blue

because

i can't

see blue

without

seeing you

(he)art.

dig in

i think

i'll always be afraid

to see you

how easily you could dig

back into my life

and how difficult

it would be

to pull you back out

the act of letting go

why do i

keep holding on to

a past love

a love that is

long gone

a love that has changed

like weather and time

a love that is inevitably

no longer mine

why am i holding on

to something

that let go

a long time ago

or in fact

never attempted

to reach out

or adjust

his grip

his hand left mine

yet i am still clenching

my fist

(he)art.

explosion

what were you thinking
trying to defuse a bomb
that already exploded
to your touch
what were you thinking
trying to stop me
from loving you too much

the fall

i told myself i would not fall for you,
so i built a barrier between us.
i wrapped my heart in caution tape and barbed wire,
anything to keep me or protect me, from you.
but i remember disneyland in december.
how you wanted to ride the bus with me.
talk for hours about absolutely anything.
how i fell in love with you on a pirate ship ride,
then you grabbed my shoulder
like it belonged to you,

like i belonged to you,

and gave me that smile that lit up
like fireworks over the magic kingdom,
thinking maybe we would have a fairytale ending.
but books have plot twists and all stories end,
and it did not matter where we left off.
whether it be on a sweet nothing
or somewhere far gone
because i knew the happiest place on earth
still would have been in your arms.

so i climbed over my walls, cut the caution tape,
and completely threw myself into the crossfire
of holding on to you and letting you go,
but i'm still trying to decide
which battle was worth fighting for.

(he)art.

where did we leave off?

i wish i had left

after the first hello

because that

would have meant

i never had to say

goodbye

but it has been

too long without you

i can't remember

our first goodbye

i can't remember

our last

homerun

in late night drives

and lustful dreams

i fell for the boy

on the baseball team

but i know he did not want

any part of me

so he left

the same way

you hit a homerun

going

going

gone

(he)art.

overplayed

your name used to be

my favorite melody

every time i sung

now it leaves

a bitter taste on me

when it dances off my tongue

holding on

maybe there's a reason

why i'm in this much pain

maybe the future ahead

is worth the wait

(he)art.

growing

through hope

and bad timing

our insides did not collide

the way i planned

i wanted to grow with you

but i suppose

we are destined to bloom

elsewhere

the way out

we always crossed paths

whether in hallways

or highways

we always went

the opposite direction

but you're only thing

i want to go towards

though life divides into freeways

and i was never supposed to

get off with you

you were an exit sign

and i had to keep going

(he)art.

zane frederick

BEATING

(he)art.

starting over

he never loved me
that's me admitting

he never stayed
i wanted committing

his actions were cruel
but they were forgiving

his leaving
was my beginning

second time around

i truly never thought

this pain would end

but i know this heart

will beat tomorrow

and i will love again

(he)art.

burn and grow

fire doesn't always

have to burn

it can be a way

to regrow

to create something new

knowing you

do not love me back

used to feel like fire

but i see flowers in me

growing slowly

maybe i could be

a garden again

more magic

though all your tricks

did not work

on him

there is still

magic in you

(he)art.

still something great

i was a sample

of something beautiful

to you

i was so tempting

so irresistible

you had to at least

have a taste

of what i had to offer

but i guess i still

wasn't good enough

and that you did not have

the courage

or bravery

to take all of me

irresponsible

you never deserved my heart

my love is golden

and i was a fool

to give it away for free

to someone who

did not want it

or in fact

did not know

what to do with it

in the first place

(he)art.

love elsewhere

no need to blame yourself

for a love he did not want

even if he didn't mean to

do not apologize

for wanting to love

something that could have been

bigger than you

do not apologize

for wanting to give love

to a carnation

that never wanted

to bloom

a natural disaster

memories of him

came in waves

and hurricanes

he was

a natural disaster

a perfect storm

an ocean

of hope

and the act

of being naive

but i do not regret

jumping in

not one bit

because i was able

to drown

and still learn

how to swim

(he)art.

graveyard of lovers

you bury your face

in your tombstone hands

because you managed to kill

all those who tried to stay

the ones who tried to love you with

the love that passed away

softer now

the feeling doesn't come in

as hot anymore

a lukewarm love

that sits in my heart

travels to my brain

settles me back

into a mindset

where reality

is as it should be

that you are gone

and not with me

(he)art.

a symphony of thoughts
fortunately

i am able

to compose a thought of you

without an entire orchestra of emotions

erupting into nervous beats

like broken piano keys

and out of tune guitar strings

now thoughts of you

come in the background

quietly

like radio silence

or elevator music

reminding me of a love

so soft and innocent

you were too afraid

to make memories out of it

but i will always remember old songs

you played in my car

how i always gave you permission

to be in charge of the aux cord

and no matter how shitty the song was

i always wanted another encore

you

were my favorite concert

sun

i am the moon

and she is the sun

you are the earth

that is in between us

and during the day

she gives you life

but when her brightness dims

i light up your night

i see she is bigger and brighter

than i will ever be

and i can see why

you want her more than me

and as you lure me in

with your gravitational pull

you make me feel like i'm spinning

in an endless black hole

and when you start to realize

that i bring you happiness

you will start to see why

she makes you lifeless

so as you orbit me

from the p.m. to the a.m.

you realize she is not the sun

i am

(he)art.

brighter

i know you have seen

my darker days

even when my flame

was lighter

but i am no longer

a dimming candle light

i'm just a little bit brighter

my own love

the love i thought
i would find
on a dead end drive
could not love me
even if he tried
this love
loved other things
with blonde hair
and blue eyes
so i try and find love
in online men
and my left hand
i understand now
i can make
my own love

(he)art.

a fixer upper

after attempting

to make a home out of you

i was able

to find a home

within myself

a fixer upper

had to repair the floors

repaint the walls

change the locks

make sure

you did not have

a spare key

to get in

the one who could not stay

you were not

the one who got away

but rather

the one who could not stay

the one

who could not handle

the love

i was trying to give you

the love

you were looking for

(he)art.

spring cleaning
you are finally
dusted out of my heart
the feelings i once had for you
have been rearranged
into poetry and months
of telling myself that
it was not meant to be
i finally moved
my bed around
made space available
inside my chest
for a lover
who will know
how to live in me
thank you for being
a lesson
thank you
for leaving

time zones
my forever
is trapped
hidden
somewhere
else
my forever
is not
with you

(he)art.

you can't hurt me anymore
i used to find comfort

and safety in you

now i find safety

and comfort

in knowing

you can

no longer

hurt me

the beach and other places

your eyes reflect like the ocean

i knew you once saw me as the sun

but now i am setting

and you are begging

for me to come home

but i have found

other front doors

and porch lights

to get lost in

i do not need your light

to feel bright anymore

(he)art.

we are bigger and better
this goes out to the homophobes
who made it seem
like being gay was a disease
that spread like a STD
for laughing at us
for our good fashion sense
and color coordination
what do you think we did
in the closet all those years?

treasure in me

there is still more of me

to discover

still more things

to fall in love with

(he)art.

plan b

i am not your midnight run

or your void to fill

your 1 a.m. replacement

or your desperate need

for validation

i'm not going to be the person

you go to when you're bored

it should be evident by now

that i am worth more

pay attention

just because

he gives you hope

does not mean

he gives you love

i know they both

look the same

but do not

confuse the two

(he)art.

fly away
stop revolving around him
stop aligning yourself
with his world
distance yourself
once you realize
there are other stars
and space to roam around
you will be free
from his gravity
start revolving
around yourself
understand
that you belong
in this space
and deserve
to be loved
in every milky way

take it or leave it

you don't get to decide

when to love me

or when to stop

you must love me

for all that i am

and all i am not

(he)art.

loud and clear

you should not

have to question

if he loves you or not

his love should come in all caps

and exclamation points

not in question marks

and lowercase

remember this

if he really was curious

he would check on you

ask if you were okay

if he really saw a future with you

he would have stayed

if he really loved you

you wouldn't feel this way

(he)art.

heavyweight memories

it's normal

to save the memories

but do not

make chains

out of them

do not allow them

to hold you down

let those days

rest in their graves

mourn those moments

if you must

but do not try

and bring them

back to life

visitors

it's okay

to let thoughts

of the person

you would like to forget

flood in

let them visit

but do not allow them

to overstay their welcome

(he)art.

home in me

i'm terrified i won't find

anyone as perfect

as i thought

i found you

but in your leaving

i found a way back

to this body

it feels good

to be home

gay pt. ii

i am gay

it sits in the back

of my throat

comfortable

in the dark

my tongue

nudges it

to come forward

launch from my teeth

show everyone

that fear

can still

look brave

(he)art.

inevitable faults of an impossible love

i cannot blame myself

for his chromosomes

did not link up with mine

he had different desires

a separate craving

for someone

of a different anatomy

i cannot change that

and i cannot align myself

with the fault

he was a boy

with good intentions

but not the ones i hoped

he was a beautiful boy

who lived in the corners of moon valley

and i hope he's smiling somewhere

i always loved him happy

adapting

i don't think

you're supposed to get over it

i believe healing

is learning to live

in the chaos

being comfortable

in vulnerable

breathing in fire

without it burning as much

being able to love

from a distance

(he)art.

in the nick of time
i like to think
you were the right person
at the wrong time
but i've come to realize
it wasn't the wrong time
just the wrong person
but when the next love comes
it won't matter the timing of it
because the right person
will control the hands of time
and the right person will hold
these fragile hands of mine

take cover

you should be afraid of me
i make thunder clap
at first glance
i shake mountains
to an avalanche
i am every hurricane
weathermen fear
you have never seen
a storm like me

(he)art.

thank you (danke schön)

you gave me everything

and nothing

and i know that's a fact

but you made me

a better writer

and i thank you for that

zane frederick

(he)art.

regret the words you didn't say.

about the author

Zane Frederick is a city born Gemini, raised in the hell and heart of Phoenix, Arizona. Poetry means absolutely everything to him, as he is captivated by turning words into stories.

With time, Zane has pridefully turned pain into poetry. He did not think a book was possible, but here it is, sitting in your hands. What used to be a daydream hobby turned into a reality. *(he)art.* is his first published book of poetry.

Zane currently attends Northern Arizona University. When not writing, he plays guitar, piano, and performs slam poetry at local coffee shops. There is still more of him to discover, more qualities to unravel and fall in love with. He has learned to love who he is and who he is still becoming.

Contact and stay connected with him:
www.zane-frederick.tumblr.com
Instagram: zane.frederick
Twitter: @zaneugh
Email: zaneschech98@gmail.com

(he)art.

21141843R00084